A VIP Day
at
Independence Park

A day behind the scenes
with a Volunteer-In-Parks
at Independence National Historical Park

by DAVID SCHWARTZ

STICKY EARTH BOOKS

Also by David Schwartz

Elsewhere Than Vietnam
A Story of the Sixties

For the
park rangers, guides,
security guards, staff,
and volunteers at
Independence National Historical Park
in Philadelphia.

Their work and dedication bring history alive.

Cover photo: *"8:59 AM". A Volunteer-in-Parks has a quiet moment with the Liberty Bell just before the doors open to admit the crowd.*

Table of Contents

Washington Square...1

Independence Hall East Wing................................5

Liberty Bell...9

Independence Hall Front Door.............................17

Independence Hall Tour...21

Independence Hall West Wing.............................41

Congress Hall Door..45

Congress Hall Tour..47

Lunch — The Bourse...59

Second Bank of the United States.......................61

Old City Hall...63

Travel Time/Carpenters' Hall..............................69

Benjamin Franklin Museum — Rear...................71

Acknowledgement..75

About the Author..77

1

Washington Square

8:20 a.m.

The number 12 city bus is almost empty by the time it reaches 8th and Locust Street where I get off. A diverse group of Philadelphians rode the bus with me through Center City: hospital workers, parents taking children to day care, students, office workers, and me in my green jacket and green shirt with National Park Service logos.

I am a "VIP" — a Volunteer-In-Parks — at Independence National Historical Park. I work there as a volunteer park ranger. Long ago I had considered becoming a history teacher, but instead I spent forty years as a Philadelphia lawyer. In retirement, I thought I could still experience teaching history. I joined the Association of Philadelphia Tour Guides, attended its lecture series, and took the exam to become a certified guide. Tour guiding is the work that I was born to do.

The bus continues on with a right turn toward Spruce Street and the Pennsylvania Hospital. Far down the block at the hospital entrance, I see an elderly woman with a walker getting out of a car.

Pennsylvania Hospital was the first public hospital in the country, founded in 1751 by Dr. Thomas Bond and Benjamin Franklin. The original brick building, the East Wing, is still in use. You can walk through the brick archway of the old carriage entrance and stroll walkways inside the walled yard. There are medicinal herb gardens and an 18th century statue of William Penn, the city's founder. You can read the faded engraving on the building cornerstone written by Franklin, that this building was "piously founded for the relief of the sick and miserable."

As prominent Philadelphia tour guide, Joe Becton, likes to say, "In Philadelphia, there is a story on every corner."

I walk a block and cross the street to enter the grassy park of Washington Square. Walking through the Square in the shade of old stately trees, I sometimes imagine I can see John Adams approaching. In April of 1777, as a delegate to the Second Continental Congress, he described walking from his boarding house at 3rd and Walnut to the Potter's field, or Strangers' Burying Ground, as the Square was then called. It served as a cemetery of unmarked graves for paupers and African-Americans. During the Revolutionary War, many soldiers from Washington's army were being buried here.

Adams wrote that evening in April to his wife Abigail, who had remained in Boston:

"I have spent an hour, this Morning, in the Congregation of the dead. I never in my whole Life was affected with so much Melancholy. The Graves of the soldiers, who have been buried in the Ground . . . dead of the small Pox, and Camp Diseases, are enough to make the Heart of stone to melt away."

Adams noted that for every soldier killed in battle, ten soldiers died of disease:

"The Sexton told me that upwards of two thousand soldiers had been buried there, and by the Appearance of the Graves and Trenches, it is most probable to me that he speaks within Bounds."

Not many people are out in the Square this early in the morning. A small group of people is exercising with slow Tai Chi poses. A few mothers walk quickly with their children in strollers. Two black labs chase a tennis ball. I approach the concrete center fountain, dry at this time of year.

To the left, the statue of George Washington comes into view beside the eternal flame commemorating the Tomb of the Unknown Soldier of the American Revolution. The square stone wall of the monument behind proclaims:

FREEDOM IS A LIGHT
FOR WHICH MANY MEN HAVE DIED IN DARKNESS

Who said that, I always ask the visitors on my walking Twilight Tours: Washington? Ben Franklin? Thomas Paine? Nobody ever guesses that this line was suggested by an unknown advertising copywriter who worked for a firm on the Square in the 1950's, when the monument was being erected.

Washington Square, Tomb of the Unknown Soldier of the American Revolution

What would I show George Washington if he miraculously appeared here one morning? It would not be the cars circling the Square or the helicopter hovering above. I imagine that I would point across the street to the building he knew as the Pennsylvania State House with the American flag waving above it. "The flag has fifty stars now," is all I would have to tell him.

I have some extra time before the 8:45 morning meeting of the park rangers and guides, so I walk up the steps of the Curtis Building, old home of the Curtis Publishing Company. I push through a heavy metal door to enter the lobby. A player piano is playing ragtime. In front of me is one of Philly's hidden gems, the huge wall mural of "The Dream Garden." It is a gorgeous mosaic of 100,000 pieces of Tiffany glass in 230 colors created over a hundred years ago by artist Maxfield Parrish and Louis Tiffany. Gardens, trees, water and mountains fill its bright landscape. The different colors of glass create the illusion of sunshine and shade, perspective and distance. It's simply beautiful. I sit on the stone bench and listen to the piano and the water trickling in the fountain.

2
Independence Hall East Wing
8:45 a.m.

I cross the street into the shady square behind Independence Hall. Before the Revolution, this historic square saw mass protests against the British and training drills of the Philadelphia militia. Now a statue of John Barry, father of the American Navy and a Philadelphian, looks down upon us.

I go in the heavy wooden door of the East Wing. At the foot of the stairway, I unhook the rope across the steps and then re-hook it after I've passed. Upstairs in the meeting room 25 park rangers and guides are sitting at long tables. I sit down next to Mike, a fellow volunteer. Mike is a former middle school history teacher and high school wrestling coach. When he speaks to school groups, he uses the best skills of both to keep their attention. Nancy, another volunteer, sits to my left. We sign in the loose-leaf notebook to record our hours worked. When we had logged 500 hours, we were given a gift pack: a Park Service water bottle, key chain, and the coveted new patch for our jackets which says "Master Ranger Corps." It is amazing how hard people will work just for a little recognition and no pay! What we really want is a ranger's wide-brimmed flat hat of our own, but volunteers don't get them.

The rangers who are the volunteer coordinators, Ted and Pete, greet us. "Thanks for coming in today," they say. A few of the rangers are reading history books as they always do. They are so knowledgeable, so good at their jobs, yet I assume greatly underpaid.

Sharon and Mary, the supervisors, stand at the front of the room. Chad, Ken and Neil sit near them at the head table doing paperwork. Mary is one of those enthusiastic managers

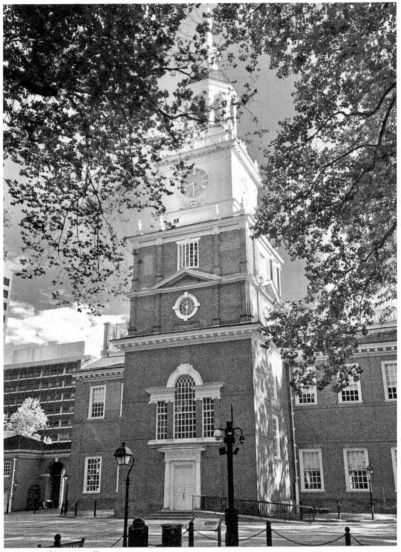

Independence Hall, rear

who likes to start meetings with a hearty "GOOD MORNING!" The group answers back with its own "Good Morning!" They announce any important people scheduled to visit the Park and any demonstrations expected. Today a Congressman will be visiting with his family at 11:00. Louis will fit in a private tour for them.

Sometimes at morning meeting a ranger gives a brief educational talk. A memorable one was Keith telling about Hannah Penn, wife of William Penn, who became governor of Pennsylvania herself after him. Keith brought in 18th century sugar cookies that he had baked to sweeten the presentation. They quickly disappeared, as do the donuts people sometimes bring in.

Ken announces whose schedules the volunteers will take today. I will be filling in for Paula. Volunteers take over a ranger or guide's regular schedule in order to free up him or her to work on special projects or attend training. One day I took Elliot's schedule so he could work on a program on Jefferson's women. Another day I substituted for Keith so he could work on a program for the Edgar Allan Poe House. Once I filled in for Penny, so she could work on the Junior Ranger Program, and another day so Nina could work on a program on Hispanic heritage.

Here comes my favorite moment of the meeting. "Thank you to all the volunteers for coming in today," Sharon says. "We couldn't keep all the buildings open and keep everything running without you. We really appreciate it." A few of the rangers and guides clap for us. This is certainly the only job I have ever had where I am thanked every single day that I come in to work!

Everyone gets up from their seats. I stand so whoever is giving me my schedule will find me. Paula comes over and gives me a small piece of paper on which she has copied over her schedule. The government does not make use of the latest scheduling technology. Our schedules are still written on paper, often recycled from discarded sample documents printed at the Franklin Court Printing Office. Maybe that is appropriate here at the Park where we celebrate the writing of the documents which founded our country. On the back of my schedule are some of the opening words from the Declaration of Independence.

VIP's usually work just part of the day. My schedule:

9:00 Bell	10:55 TT	1:00 OCH
9:50 TT	11:00 WW	2:00 TT
9:55 FD	11:45 CH Door	2:10 Rear
10:20 EW	12:00 CH Tour	3:00 Done! Thanks!
10:30 IH Tour	12:20 TT/Lunch/TT	

I take a picture of the schedule with my phone in case I lose the slip of paper! That is my use of technology for the day.

3
Liberty Bell

9:00 a.m.

I walk across Chestnut Street to the Liberty Bell Center. The Bell is visible through the large wall of glass facing the street.

I enter at a couple of minutes before 9:00. Sunlight is streaming in the high windows casting rectangles of light across the floor. The long pavilion is empty except for a couple of rangers and security staff. Already a long line of people is waiting outside the front doors. Then the doors open, and security guards begin to funnel the visitors in.

I have a stack of trading cards in my pocket to give out to kids. They resemble baseball cards, but instead have pictures and information on historic people and buildings. The kids have to "earn" a card by answering a question. To young kids I might ask, "Do you know the name of the Bell that you're going to see?" for them to earn a Liberty Bell card. To get older kids thinking, I might ask, "Why do you think it's called the Liberty Bell?" I give hints if needed – everyone has to win a card!

At the station by the front door there is a side room where we can show a twelve-minute video in eight different languages. During the busy season we might show the video to Chinese tour groups a couple of times an hour.

At the Bell itself you have to make sure people do not lean over the ropes. In all the times I have worked the Bell chamber, only once did someone suddenly reach over the rope and touch the Bell. He was a tourist from China.

"PLEASE SIR, NO TOUCHING!" I called out and walked toward him. He got the message and backed away, apologizing and bowing.

There is a crowd around the Bell, and people wait their turn to take pictures of themselves in front of the crack. We refer to these "selfie" photos here as "Bellfies".

I see Elliott is on duty here now, and there is a young woman visitor inside the ropes with him. What is she doing there?

As I come closer, I see she is holding a white-tipped cane and looking up with unseeing eyes. Sight-impaired people are allowed to touch the Bell so they can experience "seeing" it. Elliot holds her hand and is moving it over the crack in the Bell. He is reading to her the words that circle the top of the Bell:

"Proclaim Liberty throughout all the land unto all the inhabitants thereof."

Elliot has been a ranger for a long time, but he has the heart of a grandfather. I recall working the front door in Independence Hall and overhearing his talk to a large group of fourth graders. His storytelling had them mesmerized. Now I am moved to see the joy in this young woman's smile. The Bell has a magic about it that kindles the spirit of people from all over the world.

Once a student group from Israel came up to the Bell. "Shalom," I greeted them. They asked if they could take a minute to sing a song of thanksgiving and dance beside the Bell. Why not? "Go ahead, but just take a minute." Holding hands in a circle they burst into a joyous song. The other visitors enjoyed it.

Liberty Bell

When Elliott is done, I take his place beside the Bell. A school group of about thirty kids and teachers approaches now. From their blue school tee shirts, I read they are from California. I ask a teacher if they want me to talk to them, and she says that would be great.

Each ranger, guide and volunteer write their own talks. There is no canned script to follow at any of the buildings in the Park. We do borrow from each other: when I was shadowing rangers during my training, I took a lot of notes. Other facts we take from books we read or lectures we hear. There is a constant effort to improve on our interpretation. So visitors can return to the Park time after time and never hear the same talks twice.

It takes me a minute to get all of their attention, then I begin.

Welcome to the Liberty Bell. My name is Dave.

The Liberty Bell is a physical reminder of the ideals of the Declaration of Independence. Hanging in the tower of Independence Hall, which you see out the window across the street, this Bell witnessed the important events that took place there. After 90 years it cracked and was taken down, but then it emerged as a symbol of freedom for the United States, and the world. Now it's cracked and silent, but it still speaks to us.

When the Pennsylvania Assembly, or legislature, ordered a bell from England in 1751 to hang in the tower of the State House across the street, they had no idea the bell would become such a symbol. The State House then was on the outskirts of the city, and the Assembly wanted a bell for communicating with the townspeople.

Do you think there was television or internet in those days?

No, the ringing of bells had always been used to announce political meetings, to warn of danger, and to mourn for the dead. The State House bell rang to open meetings of the Assembly and to open Court sessions.

The engraving around the top of the Bell reads, "Proclaim liberty throughout all the land unto all the inhabitants thereof." These words from the Bible were most likely chosen to celebrate the 50th anniversary of William Penn's Charter of Privileges, which guaranteed religious freedom and other liberties to the cit-izens of Pennsylvania.

After the Bell arrived from London, it cracked while being tested. So two Philadelphia makers of pots and pans who had never made a bell, John Pass and John Stow, melted it down and recast it, twice. You see their names appear right here on the Bell. When England passed the Stamp Act, leading to riots in the col-onies, the Bell was rung to gather citizens to protest in the yard behind the State House. The next year it rang to celebrate the repeal of that law.

Because the wood of the State House steeple began to rot away, it became dangerous to have the heavy Bell swing back and forth to ring. So we don't know for sure if the State House Bell rang on July 8, 1776, when the Declaration of Independence was read for the first time to a crowd in the State House yard. We do know the bells of the city rang all day and into the night.

When did it become known as the Liberty Bell?

The American Anti-Slavery Society was founded in 1833. People who opposed slavery were known as abolitionists. They adopted the Liberty Bell as their symbol in a pamphlet published in 1835, saying "proclaim liberty to ALL the inhabitants" included the slaves. A description in the pamphlet of one man's visit to the bell tower was titled "The Liberty Bell."

When did it crack?

It's not known exactly when the Bell first cracked. In an attempt to fix the crack, it was drilled out and made wider, as you see. The final irreparable crack occurred in 1846 when it was ringing to celebrate Washington's birthday. The Bell was never rung again.

After the Civil War, with the abolition of slavery, the Bell traveled across the country to several world's fairs. Everywhere huge crowds came to see and cheer the Bell. The suffragists who worked for women's right to vote made their own copy of the Bell, The Women's Liberty Bell, and they put a chain around the clapper so the Bell could not be rung until women got the vote. On D-Day, the invasion of France in World War II, the mayor of Philadelphia struck the bell seven times with a mallet on national radio. Martin Luther King laid a wreath at the Bell, and each year on his birthday there is a ceremony here called "Let Freedom Ring."

On July 4, 1993, Nelson Mandela of South Africa visiting here said, "The Liberty Bell is a very significant symbol for the entire democratic world."

The American story has been a story of expanding freedom to more and more groups of people. The Liberty Bell is a symbol of that freedom. Even with its crack, the Liberty Bell looks strong and durable, but it is actually fragile and easily damaged — like freedom itself.

Independence Hall, front

4

Independence Hall Front Door

9 : 55 a.m.

I walk back across Chestnut Street to my next station, Independence Hall. Outside the back door there is a crowd in the "corral," an area encircled by fencing used to gather the ticketed visitors for the next group tour. The timed tickets are free, but must be obtained beforehand at the Visitors' Center at 6th and Market St. We take a group of up to 75 people through the building every twenty minutes. What diverse groups they are, with visitors from all over the country and the world. One day when I got home I noted down that I had spoken with people from India, Brazil, Australia, Munich, Rome, San Francisco, Nashville and Denver.

People spanning the entire political spectrum consider Independence Hall to be their own. I talk to a man in an NRA jacket, who turns out to be a history buff from Alabama. Over there is a woman in an ACLU tee shirt. For everyone, Independence Hall is a church of our civic religion. Here at the Park, people seem to set aside differences and act in a civil manner.

Gilbert is stationed to oversee the line. I love his sense of humor. Before the tour he briefs the visitors: no food or drink allowed inside, you may take photos anywhere, and please deposit your chewing gum in the trash can before entering.

"Ladies and gentlemen, I am now going to ask you to do something very difficult. To some it may sound like torture, to others merely a challenge. I ask you to turn off your cell phones now for the next half-hour. Don't worry, I promise that you all will survive!"

I head inside to relieve Libby and stand in the middle of the hallway. When the crowd starts filing in, I direct them to the Courtroom on their left. I have a clicker with which to count the number in the group. Every hour we enter the running total of visitors on a clipboard. I make sure nobody wanders away from their group.

When I am stationed at the front door some mornings there can be a few minutes when I am all alone in Independence Hall. One tour group has exited out the front door, but the next group has not yet come in the back. I walk into the Assembly Room and stand at the rail looking around at the tables. At the head table once sat John Hancock, President of the Second Continental Congress. George Washington sat there as President of the Constitutional Convention. Years later, this is the room where Abraham Lincoln's body lay in state for 24 hours on its way back to Illinois as 100,000 mourners filed by to pay their respects.

The next place on my schedule is listed as EW. We used to start Independence Hall tours with an eight-minute talk to the tour group in the East Wing annex, while they sat in folding chairs. Then we would walk them over to the front door of Independence Hall. But now we start tours in the courtroom, so visitors can enjoy their whole half hour inside Independence Hall itself.

Independence Hall, back door

Courtroom, Independence Hall

5

Independence Hall Tour

10:20 a.m.

Courtroom

The back doors swing open, and the next group comes walking in. They slow down as they are struck by the unexpected elegance of the entryway with its high ceiling, curving staircase, detailed woodwork, and light pouring through the high windows above. They suddenly realize they are in the actual building where momentous things happened.

"Folks, please move ahead to the room on your left. Please let our shorter visitors up front at the rail so everyone can see," I say a couple of times.

I try to size up the audience to gear my talk to the right level. Are there foreign visitors, so I need to speak slowly? Are there many kids, so should I ask questions to keep their attention? Is there a school group, and where are they from? For example, if they are from Delaware, I might ask them which state was the first to ratify the Constitution. Now I am ready to start.

Hello, folks. Welcome to Independence National Historical Park. My name is Dave.

We're standing here in the birthplace of the United States! In

1776, in the room across the hall, the Declaration of Independence was signed, and that was the birth of American independence from England. Then eleven years later, in 1787, delegates from 12 of the 13 states returned to that same room and wrote the U.S. Constitution. That was the birth of the American form of government, that we still live under today.

Now I said that representatives from only 12 of the states came.

Is there anyone here from Rhode Island? Rhode Island? Nobody?

They still don't show up!

The people laugh. I borrowed this line from Evan. If someone actually is there from Rhode Island, my response is, "Finally! You've shown up!"

Rhode Island was the smallest state and had no interest in being dominated in the new federal government by the large states like Virginia and Pennsylvania. Rhode Island finally ratified the Constitution three years later in 1790.

Now back in 1776, if you asked someone out on Chestnut St.: "Can you give me directions to Independence Hall?", they wouldn't have known what you were talking about. This building was known as the Pennsylvania State House: it was the capitol building of the British province of Pennsylvania. This is the original building they began to construct in 1732, the year George

Washington was born. It is almost entirely the original building: about 90% of the brickwork and about 75% of the woodwork is the original. Admire above you the work of 18th century Philadelphia craftsmen, done without modern tools.

As I said, this was the capitol building: the governor's office is upstairs, across the hall is the Assembly Room, where the elected Pennsylvania Assembly, or legislature, met, and we're standing in the courtroom of the Supreme Court of Pennsylvania.

Many Americans wanted to get rid of the King and Parliament, but they wanted to keep what worked for them, the British rule of law, represented by this courtroom. The Declaration of Independence includes a list of complaints against the King, but only one of them deals with taxes. The rest list ways the King had not followed the rule of law, for example by disbanding legislatures, ignoring charters, and depriving people of jury trials.

The British system of law was a lot like our law today. One difference — I'm standing in the dock, where the defendant or accused person had to "stand trial" — no chair in those days as he faced the judges. You were entitled to a trial by jury — you see the jury boxes. You could hire a lawyer if you could afford one — all the lawyers sat together at this table. You were entitled to a public trial — note that there are no doors on the room. The public could come in to view the proceedings just as you are.

I have watched Harriet do an interesting thing with school groups in the Courtroom to engage their minds. She divides

23

the students into two groups: she asks everyone who thinks that laws protect you to go on one side of the room. Everyone who thinks that laws limit your freedom go on the other side of the room. A lot of students want to stand in the middle, but that is not allowed. She draws out the students to explain their choice and engage in brief debate. At the end some students switch sides. She really gets them thinking.

In the years leading up to 1776, the British began imposing a series of tax laws. First came the Sugar Act, a tax on sugar, then the Stamp Act, a tax on everything made of paper. The Americans protested, and out in the State House yard where you were standing, there were large demonstrations. Thousands of people would gather to protest these laws.

They wanted to govern themselves. They argued that they had no representatives in the British Parliament 3,000 miles away in London. They didn't vote for anyone in Parliament, so they didn't consent to these laws. They thought that the only body with authority to tax them was their own Pennsylvania Assembly, whom they voted for. So the slogan of the Americans became. . .

Here I hold my hands out to encourage the group to shout, "No taxation without representation!"

In 1773 came the Tea Act, a tax on tea. The people of Philadelphia boycotted British tea. A British ship filled with tea docked down at the Delaware River, and a group of American patriot leaders visited the ship captain. They told him that for his own safety, he better turn the ship around and go back to England, which he did. But up in Boston one night, American colonists boarded a ship and threw 400 cases of British tea into the water of Boston harbor. What do we call that event today? Yes, the Boston Tea Party. To punish the people of Boston, the British closed the port — no ships in or out — disbanded the Massachu-setts legislature, and stationed troops around the city.

Now Americans in all of the colonies were angry and afraid, so all but Georgia sent representatives to meet in Philadelphia to discuss what to do. They met in Carpenters' Hall, just a block down the street at 4th and Chestnut. The building is still there, and you can visit it. They became known as the First Continental Congress. They sent a petition to the king, and the king ignored it. But they had agreed that the next spring they would meet again, and in May, 1775, when they returned, they met here in the State House, and they became known as the Second Continental Congress. When we go across the hall to the Assembly Room, we'll continue their story.

Before we go there, I want to tell you of an important event that happened in this room on July 8, 1776. All the bells of the city were ringing that morning, including possibly the State House Bell which now has a crack and is retired across the street.

I ask young children these questions:

What is the name of that bell? Now back in those days, do you think they had television? Internet?

No, it was the bells that told the people of Philadelphia that there would be an announcement in the yard at noon. A few thousand people gathered in the State House yard. At noon, out the back door walked Colonel John Nixon of the Philadelphia militia. He got up on a little stage and began to read to the people the Declaration of Independence for the first time. They had never heard it. When he was done, there was cheering, celebration, and the bells rang all afternoon.

A few men came into this room, and on the wall where there now hangs the seal of the state of Pennsylvania, at that time hung a wooden lion and unicorn, the royal coat of arms of King George III.

Here we hold up a poster of the coat of arms.

The men tore it off the wall, and dragged it through the streets. That evening a bonfire was lit as part of the celebration, and what do you think happened to the King's wooden coat of arms?

I ask the children until they get it.

Yes, they burned it, in an act of treason. Let's go across the hall now to the room where that treason was discussed.

Assembly Room

The crowd squeezes into the back area of the Assembly Room four rows deep. "There is some room in each of the corners," I announce, trying to get everyone in. The people let shorter children up front again. The visitors stay behind the bar, a wooden railing supported by vertical spindles. I see a boy is leaning on the railing with his knee pushed between two spindles.

"Please don't put your knee through there," I tell him. "This is an historic building, so if you get your leg stuck in there, we can't cut the railing to get you out!" I joke. That gets their attention! We keep a jar of Vaseline in the hall closet for cases when a leg does get stuck. It happened once to a boy on one of my tours. I started to call out to the front door person to get the Vaseline, but a teacher used a bottle of lotion in her purse to grease the leg, and the boy was saved.

Folks, welcome to the most historic room in America. This is what you came to see. The room is set up just the way it was when the Second Continental Congress arrived here in May of 1775. Each of the 13 colonies had its own table.

The month before, in April, the first shots had been fired up at Lexington and Concord in Massachusetts. The Revolutionary War had begun. So the first order of business for Congress was to choose a commander-in-chief for the Continental army. Each state had its own militia, and they had never worked together before. Fortunately, here at the Virginia table was sitting a tall man in a blue military uniform, Colonel George Washington of the Virginia militia.

John Adams, who later became our second president, was a delegate from Massachusetts. He nominated Washington to be commander-in-chief. That evening he wrote home to his wife Abigail back in Boston that when he nominated Washington, Washington jumped up and darted out of the room. He was too modest to be present when they were discussing his qualifications. Well, the Congress chose Washington, and he left for Boston to lead the army.

Assembly Room, Independence Hall

Once I had a young girl on the tour ask, "Were there any girls in the room?" She was shocked when I had to tell her that there had been only men present. After that, I began to mention Abigail Adams.

For a whole year the Congress debated what to do. Some of the men wanted to find a way to make peace with England and remain British subjects. On June 7, 1776, Richard Henry Lee of Virginia rose and proposed the resolution that "These united colonies are and by right ought to be free and independent states." Congress appointed a committee of five men to write a statement, or declaration, to the world to explain why they were taking this step of declaring independence. John Adams was on the committee, so was Ben Franklin of Pennsylvania, but they asked the youngest man on the committee, a 33-year-old lawyer from Virginia, Thomas Jefferson, to write the first draft. This walking stick here on the Virginia table belonged to Jefferson.

In 17 days, he wrote the Declaration of Independence.

I hold up a framed copy of the Declaration. But I am afraid someone might think this is the original!

This is a copy from the gift shop. It has the famous lines that all men are created equal, that we're all born with the natural right to life, liberty, and the pursuit of happiness. And that the only just government is one that governs with the consent of the people.

As modern-day citizens, it's hard for us to understand how in this room they were discussing human rights, yet many of the delegates owned slaves. Jefferson himself, who wrote in private letters about the evil of slavery, owned many slaves. He'd brought with him from Virginia to Philadelphia a 14-year-old enslaved boy, Bob Hemings, to serve as his valet. To us it's a paradox, how could smart men own slaves? But they were men of their time and place and class, and that was their world.

On the second of July, Congress passed the resolution for independence. John Adams wrote home to Abigail that the second of July will go down as a day Americans celebrate forever with parades and fireworks.

I ask a child:

But do we celebrate the second of July?

What day do we celebrate?

Yes, July 4th is our holiday, what happened?

On July 2nd, 3rd and 4th, Congress debated the Declaration of Independence and made 80 changes to it. Jefferson was not happy about that. On the 4th of July, the Declaration was approved, and that became the day we celebrate.

It's one thing to declare independence; now the Americans still had to win it from the strongest army and navy in the world, the British Empire. The Revolutionary War would continue for another long seven years. There's a line in a song in the Broadway show <u>Hamilton</u> which asks, "How does a ragtag army in need of a shower defeat a global superpower?" Well, with the leadership of the generals like Washington, the persistence of the soldiers, and a lot of help from France and the French Navy, they managed to trap the British at Yorktown in 1781 and win the war. The peace treaty was signed two years later.

Now the Americans could form the kind of government that they wanted. The states signed an agreement called the Articles of Confederation. Under the Articles, the United States was just *a loose league of friendship among 13 independent states. They intentionally made the Congress very weak. There was no President, no Supreme Court, and just one house of Congress in which each state had one vote. They did not give Congress the power to tax the people; it had to rely on contributions from the states. Congress had little money to do anything.*

One morning they looked out these windows, and they saw they were surrounded by men with rifles. These were veterans of the Revolutionary War who had never been paid, for Congress had no money to pay them. That night Congress ran away to Princeton, New Jersey, and didn't come back. Things weren't going well.

In western Massachusetts there was a rebellion of farmers, Shays' Rebellion, which closed down the courts. The call went out for the states to send representatives back to Philadelphia to fix the Articles of Confederation.

In May of 1787, representatives gathered again here in this room. They appointed George Washington to preside over what we now call the Constitutional Convention. The chair up front is the actual chair he sat in all that summer. But rather than just fix the Articles, they decided to start from scratch. With the windows closed to prevent anyone from listening in, and a guard at the door, in secret, they wrote the U.S. Constitution.

Don't think they all agreed about everything. Some men, like Alexander Hamilton, thought the President, and even the Senators, should serve for life. Only in that way would they be the equal of the kings and queens of Europe. Ben Franklin thought we should elect the president every year. Some thought that Congress should elect the President, that it was too important a job to be left to a vote of the people. Some of the men spoke of how they did not trust democracy.

The large states wanted the number of congressmen from each state to be by population, so they would have more. That seemed fair. But the small states wanted to keep it that each state had one vote, and they all were equal. The Great Compromise of the Constitution was that they agreed to have two houses of Congress: in the House of Representatives, the number of congressmen would be by population, but in the Senate, every state would have two senators, so all the states would be equal.

In September when it was time to sign the Constitution, of the original 55 delegates, only 42 were left. Some had walked out in anger or disagreement. Three of the delegates who remained dissented, so only 39 actually signed the Constitution.

As they were signing the Constitution, Ben Franklin said to those around him that all summer he'd been looking at the top of George Washington's chair, where there is half of a sun carved in it.

At this point I hold up a wooden plaque with a copy of the Rising Sun carving. I once let a blind girl run her hands over it, much like what Elliot did for the young woman at the Bell.

Franklin had worried about the future. Would the new nation fail or succeed? He said, "I have often in the course of the session looked at that sun behind the President without being able to tell whether it was rising or setting. But now at length I have the happiness to know it is a rising and not a setting sun."

Detail, chair now known as the "Rising Sun" chair (NPS Photo)

This past September we celebrated the 233rd anniversary of the signing of the Constitution. Throughout all that time, every four years, there has been a peaceful transfer of power from one administration to the next under that same Constitution. It's only been amended, or changed, 27 times. It still seems to be working.

I just want to leave you thinking about the great ideas in the most famous lines from the two great documents written here. From the Declaration, "All men are created equal." Think of the whole course of American history, and how that narrow 18th century idea of who is equal has been expanded by all the groups who have fought for equal rights. They brought about the end of slavery, the women's right to vote, and the civil rights movement. So today we say, "All people are created equal."

And from the Constitution, the first line begins, "We the people." In the first drafts it read, "We the people of New Hampshire, Massachusetts, Rhode Island, Connecticut, New York . . ." and listed the states. But in the final draft it was changed to "We the people of the United States," which shows that the authority of the federal government comes not even from the states, but from all of the people. When you think about it, the great ideas in the two great documents signed here are truly what all Americans share in common.

As I look at the visitors, I always see a couple of people who are deeply moved by the experience of being in the Assembly Room. Once in a while someone may have teary eyes. Working here can be wonderful therapy, giving perspective on whatever is happening in current politics.

In winter, we can take the much smaller groups up to see the second floor.

Now folks, today we have a special treat for you. We're going to go upstairs to see the second floor, something we aren't able to do with the summer crowds.

Second Floor

I squeeze between the people and lead them to the stairway which curves up and around to the right. The bannister is the same original thick varnished wood that Ben Franklin grasped as he went upstairs. Sunlight streams in the tall windows. At top is the famous rounded palladian window.

I let the entry area inside the Governor's office fill with people, then I begin. I point out the portrait of William Penn, founder and first governor of Pennsylvania. I have the visitors look at the floor right in front of the railing. These are the only pieces of the original floor, which have been gathered together here.

Right in front of us is what looks like an old refractor telescope on a tripod. It is the actual transit – a tool used by land surveyors – that Charles Mason and Jeremiah Dixon used to survey the Pennsylvania/Maryland border in the 1760's. That border became known as the Mason-Dixon line which separated the North from the South. A black tube on the underside is a level which still holds liquid.

I walk quickly into the Long Gallery to the end of the room and reach inside the fireplace behind the harpsichord. I push the red plastic button, and recorded harpsichord music begins to play. You can imagine you are at an 18th-century banquet here. The Long Gallery starts to fill up, and I tell the group they can sit on the benches against the walls. I point out a few of the hanging portraits. Here is Andrew Hamilton, the first "Philadelphia lawyer" who won the Peter Zenger libel case. There is a huge map of the colonies ordered from London by the Assembly's secretary, Ben Franklin, in 1732. I tell people to look closely to see it is signed and certified by mapmaker Edmund Halley, who was also the astronomer who predicted the return of Halley's comet.

I speak to the visitors.

During the Revolutionary War the British captured the city of Philadelphia and occupied it for nine months. They turned this room into a prison hospital for captured wounded American soldiers. This was during the winter of 1777–78 when Washington's army was starving in their encampment at Valley Forge, only 20 miles from where we sit. The British officers partied that winter with the daughters of Loyalist families in their warm homes.

Long Gallery, Independence Hall (NPS Photo)

I point through the windows to the National Constitution Center at the end of the Mall and recommend that people visit. Its one-person show with slides and sound, "Freedom Rising", tells the story of America in the most inspiring seventeen minutes you can spend. I also mention the new Museum of the American Revolution on 3rd Street.

The harpsichord music has finished, and it is time to leave.

We all walk down the stairs, our footsteps clattering on the wood. At the bottom of the stairs, Ralph, who is now the front door person, holds up a sign that asks for silence in eight languages, since other rangers are giving talks nearby. I hear Roy's deep bass voice coming from the Courtroom.

Then I stand outside the back door to answer questions. The next tour of Congress Hall starts in ten minutes, so I point some people in that direction.

A family from Germany asked, "Why doesn't anyone talk about Obama and Trump? We were at the museums in Washington, D.C., and they didn't there either."

"We don't talk about current politics here. It's actually against the law for us to do so," I reply.

A man once asked me after my tour, "Where was God? Why don't you mention anything about God being in the room?" We don't talk about politics or religion.

A British teacher with a class of high school girls from the London suburbs once asked me, "Who is your favorite Founding Father?" What a good question! I mulled over George Washington, Ben Franklin, Thomas Jefferson. Then I settled on my favorite: Tom Paine. His pamphlets launched the Revolution and inspired tens of thousands of citizens to keep going in the darkest hours of the war. He donated his profits from the sales of Common Sense to the soldiers' cause. His writing attacked the divine right of kings. "We have it in our power to begin the world over again," he wrote. He was an idealist who stayed true to himself and later got involved in the French Revolution. He died poor and somewhat forgotten. And he never owned a slave.

Then there was a man from China who asked me curiously, "Do you still have freedom in America?" Who knew where that question came from? What had he read in his newspapers or heard on TV back home?

"Yes, we do," I answered without hesitation. I told him how the First Amendment guarantees freedom of speech and religion and assembly.

Once as we came out of the Assembly Room a woman said, "My mother wants to know if Thomas Masaryk sat in the Rising Sun chair."

What she was referring to was, near the end of World War I, some of the now-independent Central European nations, including Czechoslovakia, Poland, Yugoslavia and others, gathered in Philadelphia to sign the Declaration of Common Aims. Inspired by the Declaration of Independence, it stated the principles of liberty which would govern their new nations. It was signed in Independence Hall. On its 100th anniversary in 2018, the original signed copy was on display here in a glass case in the West Wing.

Now of all the rangers, guides and volunteers in the Park, I just happened to be the best one to ask about Masaryk, the George Washington of Czechoslovakia. Many years ago when I was in the Army during the Cold War, I was sent to language school to learn Czech, and I interviewed refugees from Czechoslovakia for military intelligence.

"Dobry den," I say to her in Czech. "Good day." She is surprised to hear those words! After explaining how I learned to speak Czech, I tell her and her mother that I think it most likely that Masaryk did not actually sit in Washington's chair, since it is a priceless antique. I also let them know there is a historical marker about Masaryk across the street near the Wawa store. I point it out to them.

Truly, Independence Park provides inspiration for freedom to the entire world.

I have to admit that two of the most common questions we get are probably, "Where can I buy a cheesesteak?" and "How can I get to the Rocky statue?" Another is, "Where is the bathroom?" which unfortunately is a block away at the Visitors' Center. There was a bathroom building right across the street, but it's been closed for a few years.

Once a woman came up to me with questions about Hamilton. She was attending a conference at the Convention Center. She asked me to lunch (I declined). Another woman told me she wished I had been her history teacher and asked if she could hug me (I declined). Maybe it's the uniform.

Independence Hall, West Wing

6

Independence Hall West Wing

11:00 a.m.

I take the short walk next door to the West Wing, a small adjunct brick building beside Independence Hall. It displays the three important documents of the founding. Most spectacular is the actual copy of the Declaration of Independence, printed on the night of July 4, 1776, which Colonel Nixon held and read to the crowd on July 8. It was preserved by his family.

There is also the copy of the final draft of the Constitution, printed on September 15, 1787, which George Washington took with him after the Constitutional Convention. It shows a typo which was corrected in pencil. In the provision about ending the slave trade, the printer erroneously put the date that it would end in the year "one thousand seven hundred and eight" instead of the correct date twenty years into the future, 1808. The penciled correction on it was presumably made by Washington himself.

The third document is Elbridge Gerry's copy of the Articles of Confederation.

On the wall are various quotes, including Madison's words, "If men were angels, no government would be necessary."

On the other side of the room is the silver inkstand used to sign the documents, made by Philadelphia silversmith Philip Syng in 1752. I point out to kids the silver quill holder and the silver ink container.

"What is that third piece that looks like a salt shaker?" I ask. They rarely know that it held sand to sprinkle on wet ink to help it dry faster.

Once while I was here, I noticed a man and his daughter peering at the Declaration for a long time. He seemed to be reading it. He looked Chinese, so I got a Chinese brochure out of my bag for him. He thanked me in excellent English for the brochure. He said that he had memorized the Declaration to help him to learn English. He then began to recite it for me from memory! If only we could say that Americans did the same!

Lindsay comes to relieve me a few minutes early. I go outside into the bright sunlight.

On one of the benches is a mother with a few kids who are writing in their Junior Ranger booklets. These are activity books given out at the Visitors' Center for kids to enjoy. I reach into my pocket for my stack of trading cards with a rubber band around them.

"Hi, where are you from?" I ask.

They are from Texas. The mother explains that her kids are home-schooled, and they are on a family field trip. The two boys wear Civil War caps, one Union blue and one Confederate gray.

"I'll bet you were at Gettysburg yesterday," I guess, and I am right.

I start with the youngest. "Who was our first President?" The little guy looks around and holds his mother's hand.

"George Washington?" he says. It's more of a question

than an answer.

"You're right!". I give him a Washington card. "Look, he's riding his horse in the picture!"

I proceed with the other kids. "Who wrote the Declaration of Independence?" "Who was our second President?" The boys earn Jefferson and Adams cards.

I ask the daughter, "Who was our first First Lady?" She thinks for a minute. "Mrs. Washington?" With a smile I hand her the Martha card.

"Have you been in here yet?" I ask them pointing to the West Wing in front of us. They had. Now it was their turn to ask me for answers to questions in their Junior Ranger booklets.

"Why was it dark in there?" one asked.

"Why do you think?" I asked him.

"To protect the old papers," answered the older brother.

There is a lot of learning going on here at the Park.

Congress Hall Door

7
Congress Hall Door

11:45 a.m.

There is a long line outside Congress Hall. Mitch hands me the two-way radio and the clicker. There are enough seats to hold about 75 people inside, so I count on the clicker how many people are in line.

I greet the tour guide of one of the sightseeing groups we get from New York City each week. He is originally from Egypt. He has 24 people in the group. I assure him they will fit into the next tour.

"Do you have any foreign-language brochures?" he asks. "I have Italians, Spaniards, Germans, French, Israelis, and Australians." I go inside to the wooden rack to the left of the door, and get a couple of brochures in each language. This is going to be a challenging talk! I remind myself to speak slowly and use simple words.

House of Representatives, Congress Hall

8

Congress Hall Tour

12:00 p.m.

House of Representatives

The House is the large first-floor room with three horse-shoe-shaped rows of long polished wood desks. Above to the right is a gallery where the public once sat. Today's crowd fills the seats at the desks of the Congressmen. I let in a couple of last stragglers, then close the door.

Welcome to Congress Hall! My name is Dave. This is the original building, completed in 1789, where the U.S. Congress met for ten years when Philadelphia was the capital of the United States from December, 1790 to 1800. During those ten years they were building the new capital city of Washington, D.C. This room was the House of Representatives, and in a few minutes we'll go upstairs to see the Senate. The chair up front is one of four original chairs from the 1790's. One of the chairs was used by the Speaker of the House in this room, and another was used by the Vice President, upstairs in the Senate. A third chair is located in Old City Hall, the building at the corner on the other side of Independence Hall. The Chief Justice used the chair in that building where the Supreme Court met. Because the chairs are identical, we do not now know exactly which chair belongs in which room.

47

The building was built to be the Philadelphia county court-house. But when the federal government moved to Philadelphia after just a year and a half in New York City, which was the first capital, Philadelphia lent Congress the use of this courthouse building. They knew that the federal government would just be here temporarily, for ten years, so the city did not build new buildings, but just lent them what they had.

We don't know exactly how the Congressmen arranged themselves to sit, but on one day a congressman did draw up a seating chart to show where everyone was sitting. James Madison, the well-respected Father of the Constitution from Virginia, was sitting here in the first seat in the first row — closest to the fireplace.

The boy sitting in that chair smiles.

Although the Constitution had been ratified in 1788, there was still no real sense yet of American nationalism. People considered their state was their country: they were New Yorkers, Pennsylvanians, Virginians. The states competed with each other, they each had their own militia or army, even their own navy, they each printed their own money. When it came to ratifying the Constitution, with its new stronger central government, almost half the country was against it. But after ten years of working together in this room, in 1800 when Congress left for Washington, D.C., you could say everyone now agreed that the Constitution was the highest law of the land, and that they thought of themselves as Americans.

One of the tests of the new government during those years was the Whiskey Rebellion in 1794. Congress passed a tax on whiskey. The farmers in western Pennsylvania and what is now Kentucky refused to pay it. They did not recognize the power of the new federal government to tax them. President Washington had to send an army to put down the rebellion, which it did without firing a shot.

One of the most important things that happened in this room was not anticipated by the Founders, and that was the development of the first two political parties. The Founders did not like political parties, which they had called "factions." But two factions began to emerge. On one side were the Federalists, who included Vice President John Adams and Alexander Hamilton, secretary of the treasury. The Federalists favored a strong central government to unite the 13 states and make the U.S. one strong nation, the equal of England or France.

On the other side were the Democratic-Republicans, who included Thomas Jefferson, the secretary of state, and James Madison, the representative from Virginia. The Democratic-Republicans, mainly Southerners, favored states' rights, that the federal government should not do anything more than what was listed in the Constitution, and the states would control everything else. When you think about the course of American history, that debate continues right up through today: how much power should the federal government have, and how much power should be left to the states.

One important issue had been over Hamilton's financial and economic plans for the country, dramatized in the Broadway show Hamilton. During the Revolution the states had borrowed a lot of money which they now couldn't repay, so the U.S. had very poor credit. Hamilton's plan was to have the federal government take over and repay the debts of the states. Finally his opponents agreed to it, in return for the new capital of the country being in the South. That's when they began to build the new city of Washington, D.C., and the capital moved temporarily to Philadelphia for ten years.

Now Hamilton wanted to create a national bank to stabilize the economy. His opponents argued no, there's nothing in the Constitution about creating a national bank. But they finally agreed to Hamilton's plan, and Hamilton personally convinced Washington to sign the bill. Congress also created the first U.S Mint here in Philadelphia, to print one form of currency that would be used throughout the country.

I have seen Jody do a terrific job with student groups here in Congress Hall. She asks them questions which have them vote and make decisions as if they were Congressmen of that time. If you were a representative from Virginia, which had already paid off its war debt, would you vote to contribute to paying off the war debt of another state, like Massachusetts? At the end of her talk in the House, she tells the students they have now been elected to the Senate, so everyone heads upstairs.

During the ten years here the Bill of Rights was ratified by the states and became law. Those are the first ten amendments to the Constitution which guarantee many freedoms. Can anyone tell me one of them? Freedom of religion. Freedom of speech. Freedom of the press. Yet in 1798 Congress passed the Alien and Sedition Acts, which made it a crime to criticize the President or the government. Some newspaper editors were actually thrown in jail for that. One editor called Adams "a pompous clown" and was arrested.

In northern states like Pennsylvania, laws were being passed to gradually abolish slavery, but here in this room Congress passed the Fugitive Slave Act, making it a crime to help a runaway slave.

One day in 1798 a dispute between Federalist Roger Griswold and Matthew Lyon, a Democratic-Republican, erupted into an actual fight. Griswold began to hit Lyon with his cane, and Lyon grabbed the fireplace tongs. They had to be separated by other Congressmen. Here is a poster of a political cartoon from a newspaper of that day illustrating the fight.

Historians tell us that the most important event to occur in this room was the inauguration of John Adams to be the second president. George Washington was elected twice, and nobody ran against him. But Washington decided he would not run for a third term. He felt if he did that it would become a lifetime job, and he would be like a king.

So in 1796, there was the first contested American election

for President. John Adams, the Federalist, ran against Thomas Jefferson, the Democratic-Republican. It was a very close election, and Adams won by just three electoral votes. Picture this room on March 4, 1797. The seats were filled with the Congressmen. The Senators came down from upstairs with their chairs and were sitting here. President Washington had the seat of honor here. Up in the gallery with the newspapermen were observers from Europe who didn't believe that the United States could succeed. How could you have a country with no king? King George III of England had once said, if Washington voluntarily gives up his power, then he's the greatest man in the world. No king in Europe had ever done that.

At noon, in the door came John Adams, the new President, and Thomas Jefferson, the new Vice-President. Originally, the Constitution provided that whoever got the second-most votes became Vice-President. They didn't anticipate the development of political parties. So we had as president John Adams the Federalist, and as vice-president Thomas Jefferson, the Democratic-Republican, and they did not particularly like each other. The Constitution was changed soon after that, so that won't happen again. The Electoral College now votes separately for a president and a vice-president.

On that day, John Adams made a short speech and took the oath of office right here. It was the first peaceful transition of power from one man to the next by means of an election in modern history. It showed that the new Constitution would work.

Senate

We'll go upstairs to the Senate now. Please watch your step going upstairs. You are going to walk past committee rooms where small groups of Senators did their work. In the last two rooms are large portraits of the king and queen of France, Louis XVI and Marie Antoinette, which were gifts from France after the Revolutionary War. I want one of you students to tell me upstairs why the portraits are there. I'll meet you at the end of the hall in the Senate chamber.

I lead them up the steep stairs. Not long ago, I had a large group of Chinese tourists up here. I would say a few lines in English, and their Chinese tour guide would translate. I asked the guide where in China they were from.

"New York City," he answered with a smile. That's America.

Upstairs as the visitors file past the committee rooms, I point out the legal documents on tables tied with red ribbons.

Notice that they used to tie up legal documents with red ribbons around them, which years later gave rise to the phrase "tied up in red tape" to mean slow bureaucratic government action. Here are the portraits, yes, given because France was an ally of the United States during the Revolution. The original portraits were lost or destroyed. These reproductions were given to us by France in 1976 to celebrate the Bicentennial.

This last committee room was where the first Library of Congress was located, signified by those book shelves. Today the Library of Congress has over 39 million books.

Senate, Congress Hall (NPS Photo)

We are standing now in the Senate chamber. Note how elegant this room appears with its red curtains, green walls, and carpet compared to the House downstairs. The chair up front is the original chair from the 1790's. Who sat in that chair to preside over the Senate? Yes, the Vice-President. So John Adams and then Thomas Jefferson sat there. George Washington's second inauguration took place here. His inauguration speech that day was only 135 words, the shortest in history.

Compare the Senate chamber to the House downstairs, and you physically see the Great Compromise of the Constitution. The large states wanted the number of congressmen for each state to be according to population, so the large states would have more. That seemed fair to them. But the small states like Delaware and New Jersey wanted each state to continue to have one vote in Congress, so they would all be equal. The Great Compromise was that we would have two houses of Congress: downstairs in the House it would be by population, and here in the Senate every state would have two senators, even the small states, so they would all be equal.

More than 20 of the other 32 chairs here are original. 32? Shouldn't there be 26, two for each of the 13 states? What happened? During the ten years here, three new states joined the union: Vermont, Kentucky and Tennessee. Andrew Jackson, who later became president, sat here as one of the first Senators from Tennessee. James Monroe, our fifth President, also sat here as a senator from Virginia.

Originally under the Constitution, people did not vote for Senators like we do today. Senators were selected by each state legislature. This was not changed until the 17th Amendment to the Constitution in 1913 when people began voting directly for their Senators.

Originally the Senate met in secret. After five years of pressure from the press and public they built the gallery over our heads, so people could come in and hear what their senators were saying.

This copy of the original carpet, made in Philadelphia, has the large seal of the United States, surrounded by the interlocking seals of the original 13 states. Senators were criticized in the newspapers for spending so much money on this carpet and the other furnishings.

The pictures on the walls are of the battle of Quebec, and the Battle of Bunker Hill in the Revolutionary War.

Adams was the first vice president to say that the vice presidency is "the most insignificant office that ever the imagination of man conceived." The main job of the vice president, other than to serve if something happens to the president, is to vote to break a tie vote in the Senate. To show how divided the country was right from the beginning between the two political parties that were developing, Adams had to vote to break a tie 29 times, far more than any vice-president except John Calhoun in the 1820's.

Congress Hall is the oldest building still standing which was once used by the U.S. Congress. We have seen how some things were different in the early years of our government, but also how many things have remained the same. The American experiment in democratic self-government has been a success.

That ends our tour. Please watch your step going down the stairs, and have a great visit.

Independence Hall, West Side

The Philadelphia Bourse Building

9

Lunch — The Bourse

12:20 p.m.

The morning meeting room doubles as a lunch room. I love being among the rangers. One memorable April day I joined a few of them on a field trip which Louis planned to Harriton House in Bryn Mawr. Stan, Jody, Nina and Sally went along too. Harriton House, built in 1704, was the country home of Charles Thomson, secretary of the Continental Congress. Together we stood over Thomson's original writing desk on display. Imagine the men who had stood in front of that desk, and the papers that had rested on it! Afterwards, we had lunch in Ardmore.

Today is a nice day to eat outside. I walk half a block up 5th Street to The Bourse food court. The Bourse is a beautiful golden stone building from 1895 that was originally a commodities exchange. Now it is an office building with a food court in the central atrium. Today I get a sandwich to go from Rustica, and I walk outside to a park area to sit on a stone bench.

The Second Bank of the United States looms behind me. I walk close by here when leading my Twilight Tours in summer. Those walking tours are free, led by volunteers, and leave from the Visitors' Center every summer evening at 6:00. I take my groups on a route behind Independence Hall and the Second

Bank, past this spot, staying in the shade of the old trees. On a hot Philly night there is no cooler, quieter place in the city.

Second Bank of the United States

10

Second Bank of the United States

12:20 pm

The Second Bank is a huge edifice of Pennsylvania marble with wide steps from the sidewalk up to the entrance between tall marble columns. It was modeled after the Parthenon in Athens. The building was completed in 1824 when Greek revival architecture was in vogue. It replaced Hamilton's First Bank of the U.S., built in 1795, which still stands a block away and was the first American central bank. Today, the First Bank is part of Independence Park but is closed.

The Second Bank behind me is open to visitors. Its rooms hold a portrait gallery of the Founders and other prominent men and women of 18th century America. Many of the paintings were done by Charles Willson Peale. He never saw a painting until he was 21, and at that moment he determined to study art. Peale created the first museum in America, which for a time was on the second floor of Independence Hall. Besides the portraits, his museum held many items of natural history, including fossils and taxidermy animals. You can still see his mounted pet eagle on display at the Bank.

I remember observing Evan teaching a young school group how to read the information about a painting on the plaque beneath it: the name of the artist, the year the painting was done, and the years of birth and death of the person painted. "How do you think Charles Willson Peale painted this self-portrait of himself?" Eric would ask. And the classic scavenger hunt question, "Find the one portrait in here of a man with a moustache and come back and tell me who he was and something about him."

Now it is time for me to head back a block to Old City Hall at 5th and Chestnut.

Independence Hall, foreground, and Old City Hall, background

11

Old City Hall

1:00 p.m.

It is easy for visitors to the Park to miss Old City Hall. If the front door with the metal bolt latch stays closed, few people come in. The small plaques on the wall outside do not really broadcast the historical importance of the building. But if it's a hot day and the door gets left open, people pour in thinking this is the entrance of Independence Hall.

On the way in I passed the open door of the gift shop, which has no customers at the moment.

Now I am sitting on a bench against the back wall of the courtroom, alone, facing the empty judges' chairs up front. We give no group tours here. It is an open house: when people come in, we explain the room to them.

Hi, folks. Welcome to Old City Hall. My name is Dave. This is the original building from 1791 built to be Philadelphia City Hall, but during the ten years that Philadelphia was the capital of the U.S., this is the courtroom where the U.S. Supreme Court met. That was from 1791 to 1800, when they were building the new capital city of Washington, D.C.

The Supreme Court did not have many cases in the early years, so the Court was in session only for two weeks in February and two weeks in August. During the rest of the year, this was the Philadelphia city courtroom. That is why we have the wooden box of the dock here, where the defendant "stood trial" — no chair for him in those days. To the left is the jury box with three rows of wooden benches. In front of the chairs of the justices is the witness box, and all the lawyers sat around the same table in the center.

As I sit alone, I reach under the bench and pull out one of the loose-leaf notebooks filled with information about the early Supreme Court. In this courtroom we discuss Supreme Court cases and the rule of law.

Once I had the room packed with a school group from California. Joe Becton, the Philly tour guide, had herded them in with his usual enthusiasm. Joe is a tall African-American who wears the uniform of a black soldier of the Revolutionary War, of whom there were thousands.

"Philadelphia is associated with freedom," Joe told his students here in the Supreme Court chamber.

I picture Alexander Hamilton and John Marshall arguing cases before the Supreme Court in this room. I recall that I was sitting here on one of the days that the nomination of Justice Kavanaugh was being debated in the Senate.

A family comes in for the gift shop. I tell them to come back into the courtroom first, it will just take a couple of minutes. They are from Dayton, Ohio. "Can I take pictures?" the dad asks. "Sure."

Courtroom, Old City Hall

The tall chair in the middle is one of four original chairs from the 1790's. One of these chairs was used by the Chief Justice in this room. The first Chief Justice was John Jay of New York. Two of those chairs are over in Congress Hall, where one was used by the Speaker of the House, and the other by the Vice-President. Because the chairs are identical, we do not now know exactly which chair belongs in which room.

Kids, count for me how many chairs we have up front? Yes, six! Today we have nine justices on the Supreme Court, but originally there were only six — an even number! Today we think that would be crazy, because you could have a three-to-three tie decision.

Because there were no separate Circuit Court judges appointed like today, Supreme Court justices had to travel much of the year and serve as Circuit Court judges together with the District Court judges. This was called "riding circuit." Because of all the travel by horse and carriage, in all kinds of weather, staying at inns where they would have to share a room, Supreme Court justice was not a great job. Even though the Constitution provides that Supreme Court justices are appointed for life, almost all of them quit within just a few years. John Jay left to become governor of New York.

There were no famous cases you would have heard of during the ten years here. Perhaps the most well-known case was Chisholm v. Georgia (1793). A resident of South Carolina sued the state of Georgia to be repaid money he had lent to Georgia for the Revolutionary War. Georgia could not pay back the debt and claimed that a state was protected from being sued by a citizen of a different state in federal court. The Supreme Court held that Georgia did owe the money, but Georgia still refused to pay. This decision resulted in passage of the Eleventh Amendment the next year, which provides that a resident of one state cannot sue another state in federal court.

Here in this modest room, the Supreme Court heard its first cases and began its work of shaping the American justice system.

"Do you have tickets for the Independence Hall tour?" I ask them.
"Yes, for 2:20."
"Perfect. There are two other buildings in the Square where you can spend some time before your tour. Go through security next door. The West Wing, which is the small building

on the other side of Independence Hall, has some original documents. And Congress Hall on the far corner is where Congress met when Philadelphia was the capital. The next tour there starts at 1:40, so you'll be out by 2:00."

They thank me, and they are off.

Carpenters' Hall

12
Travel Time/Carpenters' Hall

2:00

Walking down Chestnut Street toward the Ben Franklin Museum I pass the Second Bank of the United States again, and at 4th Street the brick Pemberton House, a reconstruction of a home of a wealthy Quaker merchant. Inside is the office of the Independence Historical Trust, which sponsors the free walking Twilight Tours. Behind it is Carpenters' Hall.

In September, 1774, the First Continental Congress, comprised of delegates from twelve of the American Colonies, convened here. They planned joint action against the British, who had closed the port of Boston to punish the colonists for the Boston Tea Party. This group of leaders, which included George Washington, John Adams, Sam Adams, and John Jay among others, rented the newly-completed meeting hall of the Carpenters' Company, which was a trade guild of master builders. The Congress agreed to begin a boycott of all British goods in the next year.

It was here that Patrick Henry rose and gave a stirring speech that moved the Colonies down the road toward independence. "British oppression," he said, "has effaced the boundaries of the several colonies; the distinctions between Virginians, Pennsylvanians and New Englanders are no more. I am not a Virginian, but an American."

Ben Franklin with Ryan on the University of Pennsylvania campus.

13

Benjamin Franklin Museum — Rear

2:10

I cross the street and enter the alley which opens into Franklin Court. The reconstructed beams of Franklin's house rise before me.

Ahead are the backs of the brick townhouses which hold the post office and the printing shop. Park rangers give a demonstration of 18th century printing techniques with a replica of a printing press that Franklin used. They set the old metal type and print copies of the Declaration of Independence and other early documents. Jason showed me how as he set up one morning before school groups began to arrive. Ink is applied by pounding on the type with leather ink balls that look like boxing gloves. Then damp rag paper is placed over the type and gets pressed tightly against it.

I enter the museum and go down the stairs. The rear ranger station is in the main museum room below ground level. The Museum holds displays in plexiglass cases that tell the story of Franklin's life and his achievements. In the middle of the room is a timeline listing his accomplishments from each decade. He founded the first American public library, the first fire insurance company, the American Philosophical Society to advance scientific knowledge, and the Academy and

College of Philadelphia, which developed into the University of Pennsylvania.

There are quotes by Franklin throughout the room, as "Life is a kind of chess," next to an 18th century chess set. There are displays of his inventions, beginning with wooden swim fins which he invented when he was a boy, followed by bifocal glasses, the Franklin stove, and his experiments with electricity. From late in his life when Franklin was unable to walk far, there is a French sedan chair similar to the one in which he was carried to the Constitutional Convention each morning by four prisoners from the Walnut Street jail.

There are lots of hands-on displays for kids. On days when a school group comes in, I need to be alert, as the students can be rough on the exhibits they handle.

At a few minutes before 3:00, here comes Gilbert to relieve me.

"Well, Mr. Schwartz, are we going to have a peaceful transfer of power here?" he asks with his smile.

So another great day as a VIP ends with a laugh.

"Thanks for coming in, David," Gilbert adds. "See you next week."

I walk back up Chestnut Street, and take 5th St. over to Walnut to catch the number 12 bus home. I am following in the footsteps of our Founding Fathers who walked these same cobblestone streets. Today I played a little part in keeping their history alive.

As a VIP — a Volunteer in Parks — I have been thanked for the Declaration of Independence by a couple from Argentina. They told me that they wanted to thank the Founders, and I was here as their representative. I have sat with a young woman from Amsterdam explaining how our elections work compared to their parliamentary system with its many political parties. I have spoken with Chinese college exchange students who translate my words to their parents visiting from China who speak no English. More than once I have had a young boy recite all the names of the Presidents in order in a little memorized song.

A man from Rwanda shook my hand to tell me his visit to Independence Hall was the culmination of a life-long dream. He knew American history and loved all the best that America stands for in the world. I have met visitors from almost every state in the union and helped them to enjoy their visits to Philadelphia. It is an honor to work here with the rangers and guides at Independence Park — The Greatest Park in History.

Acknowledgement

I would like to acknowledge the excellent book <u>Independence: A Guide to Historic Philadelphia</u> by George W. Boudreau (Westholme Publishing, LLC, 2012). I have relied on it for my talks as a VIP and as a walking Twilight Tour guide. George's block-by-block description of historic Philadelphia is invaluable for any tourist or tour guide.

About the Author

David Schwartz at Independence Hall on National Parks Service day with Buddy Bison, mascot of the National Parks Trust.

David Schwartz is a Volunteer in Parks (VIP) at Independence National Historical Park in Philadelphia, serving as a volunteer park ranger and greeting visitors from all over the world. He also volunteers to lead free walking Twilight Tours on summer evenings. He is a certified tour guide and member of the Association of Philadelphia Tour Guides.

David became a VIP in retirement, after a career as a Philadelphia lawyer. He lives with his wife Maryellen in the historic Naval Square neighborhood.

He is the author of a novel, <u>Elsewhere Than Vietnam: A Story of the Sixties</u>, based on his experiences in the U.S. Army.

Made in the USA
Middletown, DE
23 March 2022

63009963R00050